Ways to Shiva

Published on the occasion of the exhibition
"Manifestations of Shiva,"
organized by the Philadelphia Museum of Art

This publication has been made possible by a grant from the
National Endowment for the Humanities, a Federal agency

Ways to Shiva

LIFE AND RITUAL IN HINDU INDIA

Joseph M. Dye

PHILADELPHIA MUSEUM OF ART

COVER:
On a small altar at the foot of a tree in the city of Benares rests
a stone linga, the sign or symbol of the Hindu god Shiva. This
shrine lies near fields of golden marigolds that are gathered to
make flower garlands for the city's temples. Each day, the
marigold pickers decorate this little shrine with some flowers
from their harvest as an offering to Shiva and to the spirit that
inhabits the tree.

Manifestations of Shiva

Philadelphia Museum of Art
March 29–June 7, 1981

Kimbell Art Museum, Fort Worth
August 1–September 27, 1981

Seattle Art Museum
November 25, 1981–January 31, 1982

Los Angeles County Museum of Art
March 18–May 30, 1982

Editor: George H. Marcus
Designer: Joseph B. Del Valle
Printer: Lebanon Valley Offset

Library of Congress Cataloging in Publication Data
Dye, Joseph M   1945–
Ways to Shiva.
Bibliography: p. 95
1. India—Religious life and customs.   2. Siva
(Hindu deity)—Cult.   I. Title.
BL2001.2.D93   294.5   80-25113
ISBN 0-87633-038-3

Foreword

There are many ways to Shiva, and many very different encounters with this paradoxical Hindu god. Like most Westerners, I was first conscious of Shiva as a bronze image—that of the cosmic dancer—in a museum. His four arms were in movement, his gestures delicate, his legs powerful, his face enigmatic—the whole surrounded by a mandorla of flames. He was illusive and provocative, and this led me to read a book of essays on Indian art by the late Ananda Coomaraswamy, *The Dance of Śiva.** I read: "In the night of Brahmā, Nature is inert, and cannot dance till Śiva wills it: He rises from His rapture, and dancing sends through inert matter pulsing waves of awakening sound, and lo! matter also dances appearing as a glory round about Him." From the words of Coomaraswamy, I was able to understand Shiva as a symbol of energy. Later, in reading *An Area of Darkness* by the Trinidadian author V.S. Naipaul, I was able to appreciate the despairing words of a man who in tracing his own roots in India, wrote at one moment during his travels: "Shiva has ceased to dance."

When I came to the Philadelphia Museum of Art as its Director in 1979, I discovered that this was not so. Shiva was indeed still dancing, and not only through the will of its Curator of Indian Art, Stella Kramrisch. She was completing a book about the complex nature of Shiva *(The Presence of Śiva)* and preparing an exhibition, "Manifestations of Shiva," to

*"Shiva," according to an alternate system of transliteration

6

show how Indian artists have conceived of this god over some two thousand years. It was through her that I discovered in what a bewildering number of forms besides the Lord of the Dance that Shiva has made himself manifest.

I was fortunate to be able to go to India through the graces of the Indo-U.S. Subcommission on Education and Culture and I made the inevitable pilgrimage to the island of Elephanta in the harbor of Bombay. There, I found represented in gigantic rock-cut sculpture, various episodes from the mythology of Shiva, but most awe-inspiringly, on one of the axes of the shrine, I saw, enshrouded in half-light, the profound triple heads of Shiva, the Great God, a serene, unmoving presence. I saw other great representations of Shiva—bronze figures in the museum in Madras, the reliefs of the temples of Mamalla-puram and Kanchipuram, the great sculptures in the rock-cut temple of Kailasanatha in Ellora. But what was more signifi-cant was that I saw people worshiping Shiva, in temples—for example, in a colorful new sanctuary in Madras—as well as through the ordinary actions of their everyday lives. In India, as we are often told, there is genuinely no distinction between the sacred and the profane.

This book is intended to give works of sculpture and paintings devoted to Shiva, which we might find in a museum, a private collection, or in India itself, a human dimension. In showing what Shiva means as the organizing principle of the lives of many Indians, its author, Joseph M. Dye, helps make the East less remote for Westerners and helps us understand more clearly that part of the globe inhabited by one-seventh of the world's population.

Dr. Dye is Curator of Asiatic Art at the Virginia Museum of Fine Arts. In writing this book, he has had as a guide Stella Kramrisch, his former professor at the Institute of Fine Arts, New York University, and as an adviser, George H. Marcus, Head of Publications at the Philadelphia Museum of Art. Most significantly, *Ways to Shiva* has grown out of his long discus-sions with many Indian friends and his intimate knowledge and deep understanding of India and its people.

Jean Sutherland Boggs
Director

India:
The
Setting

Once you have experienced India, you cannot forget it. A dusty train in Rajasthan, a fragment of conversation at a tea stand, the ecstatic fervor of a religious procession in Benares, a glimpse of the Himalayas—the overwhelming diversity of the country returns in a series of sharp, powerful images. Few nations on earth are as complex or as baffling. The India of today is a highly industrialized country, and yet, it embraces one of the world's oldest traditional cultures. In the cities of New Delhi, Bombay, Calcutta, and Madras, fluent English, Western clothes, nightclubs, department stores, and movies are part of many people's lives. But not so many miles away, in rural villages, a timeless existence endures just as it has for thousands of years. The fields are still tilled with wooden plows pulled by oxen; people live in mud houses illuminated by oil lamps, and draw their water from village wells, their lives dominated by the course of the seasons, the sunrise and sunset, and the spirits that dwell in trees and ponds. And beyond the villages, beyond the farms, in even more remote areas, are separate tribal cultures with religions, rites, and languages all their own.

The people of India inhabit a country so large that it is considered a subcontinent, extending more than two thousand miles from the almost impenetrable northern barrier of the Himalayas to the long, sandy coastline of the south. Within its borders are arid deserts, tropical rain forests, lofty snow-covered mountains, and wide flat plains and plateaus. This spacious

Garlands of marigolds, piled high in mounds at a market in Benares, are sold for presentation to one's guests and for offerings to the gods.

AFGHANISTAN

PAKISTAN

Cities and Sites

| 0 | 100 | 200 | 300 MILES |
| 0 | 100 | 200 | 300 KILOMETERS |

CHINA

JAMMU AND
KASHMIR

Srinagar • •Amarnath

Jhelum

Chenab

Kangra
Guler • HIMACHAL
Mandi• PRADESH

Ravi

Beas

Harappa •

PUNJAB

Sutlej

Indus

Mohenjo-
Daro •

Kedarnath •

•Kailasa

T I B E T

Brahmaputra

HARYANA

New Delhi •
DELHI

UTTAR
PRADESH

NEPAL

H I M A L A Y A

SIKKIM

S

BHUTAN

ARUNACHAL
PRADESH

ASSAM

NAGA-
LAND

RAJASTHAN

•Jaipur

Chambal

Jamuna

Benares •

Ganges

MEGHALAYA

MANI-
PUR

•Jodhpur

BIHAR

BANGLADESH

TRIPURA

MIZO-
RAM

• Karachi

Udaipur •

Khajuraho •

Dacca •

GUJARAT

MADHYA PRADESH

• Deogarh

WEST
BENGAL

Calcutta •

I N D I A

Narbada

ORISSA

BURMA

Tapti

• Nasik

MAHARASHTRA

Godavari

Mahanadi

Elephanta

Bombay •

ANDHRA PRADESH

A R A B I A N

S E A

Aihole •

Krishna

Pattadakal •

Tungabhadra

BAY OF BENGAL

KARNATAKA

• Madras

• Halebid

• Kanchipuram

• Tiruvannamalai

• Chidambaram

TAMIL

• Tanjore

KERALA

NADU

• Madura

• Rameshwaram

SRI
LANKA

I N D I A N   O C E A N

Jean Paul Tremblay

landscape is washed by many great rivers, among them the sacred Ganges, which waters the fertile plains of northern India.

The climate of India is as variable as its landscape, but essentially it is tropical. Even in the north, where the autumn and winter are cool, and clear skies and sunshine may last for weeks or sometimes for months, the weather can be relentless and overpowering. March brings the dry heat of summer throughout most of the country: a hot wind blows almost continuously, temperatures reach as high as 120 degrees Fahrenheit, and the land becomes parched. Life nearly ceases. All of India waits expectantly for the relief of the monsoons, the torrential rains that can once again make the countryside lush and green. If they come, the harvest will be good; if not, drought and possibly famine will follow.

Like other aspects of India, her religions and languages are numerous and varied. Hinduism, the faith of the majority of the population, is followed by about 500 million of the country's 630 million people. There are also Muslims (India's largest religious minority), Christians, Sikhs, Buddhists, Jains, Parsis, and Jews. India's declared national language is Hindi, a language that originated in northern India, but some fourteen other major languages and hundreds of dialects, as well as English, are also widely spoken.

The traditional culture that underpins life in this vast and diverse country reaches back to at least 2500 B.C., when what is known today as the Indus Valley culture—one of the world's earliest civilizations—was at its height. Its life was centered in large cities such as Harappa and Mohenjo-Daro (both located near the Indus River valley in modern-day Pakistan). These cities were laid out according to unusually systematic plans, which incorporated remarkably advanced bathing and hygienic facili-ties, suggesting that rigorous order and purity must have been quite important to this culture. Their religion seems to have been concerned with the generative powers of nature: many carved stone seals and clay figurines found in the Indus Valley depict bulls, tigers, elephants, and other animals of great physical and sexual energy, while Indus "mother goddess" figurines with their large hips and breasts are equally suggestive of a concern for fertility.

Like the streets of such crowded cities as Benares (top left), modern India is a complex mixture of many different ways of life, but certain common realities dominate the country. India is primarily a land of farms and small villages—a world of simple houses (top center) and communal wells (middle left), such as these in Rajasthan. Life in these villages—indeed throughout the whole of India—is dominated by agriculture, and by the appearance of the monsoon rains shown here flooding the streets of Benares (middle right). If the monsoon comes, crops such as the rice being transplanted near Madras (lower left) will grow and India's enormous population will be fed. Many Indians are vegetarians, and reverence for all forms of life is profound: some people (top right) dispose of their dead farm animals as they would members of their family—by carrying them to a river, although the carcasses are not cremated but merely cast into the water.

Suddenly, in about 1500 B.C., the Indus civilization collapsed, and the cities were abandoned. No one knows exactly why. The loosely organized villages that continued preserved parts of its culture, but sometime before 1000 B.C. they were conquered by nomadic Aryan tribes, whose homeland was far to the northwest, near the Caspian Sea. The impact that the Aryans and their successors made on Indian civilization was overwhelming. Among the most pervasive innovations was the division of all Indian society into four social classes determined by birth: Brahmans, or priests; Kshatriyas, or warriors and rulers; Vaish-

yas, or merchants and farmers; and Shudras, or servants. The Brahmans were regarded as the first and highest class; directly under them in social importance were the Kshatriyas, then the Vaishyas, and finally the Shudras.

Centuries after the Aryan invasions, there arose alongside and within these four broad classes lesser social divisions, or castes, based primarily upon occupations. The rank of each caste depended upon the supposed antiquity of its origin, the ritual purity of its members, and the recognition of its position by other groups. Elaborate and strictly observed rules carefully regulated all aspects of daily life, including the interchange of food, water, and services among different castes. This all-encompassing system of social organization, although officially discouraged, still regulates life in India today.

If the Indus peoples seem to have worshiped powers embodied within the physical forms of nature, their conquerors, the Aryans, believed that there were certain divine powers, or gods, who represented and exercised control over nature's many forms. Among the most important Aryan deities were Agni, god of fire, and Indra, chief of the gods; however, it was two relatively minor Aryan gods—Vishnu, a divinity often associated with the sun, and Rudra, the Great Archer, and bestower of healing herbs—who would assume importance in later Indian religion. Preeminent among Aryan religious rituals was the fire sacrifice, which in its earliest stages was regarded as a rite of hospitality to the gods: they were invited to a fire built upon a special altar, honored with

The landscape of India is as diverse as its many peoples, religions, and languages. The country contains not only great metropolises, such as Calcutta (upper left) with its high-rise structures and stately, columned buildings, but also thousands of villages of mud-brick houses, such as these in Madhya Pradesh (lower right). India is bordered on the north by the majestic, snow-covered Himalayas, the traditional abode of Hindu holy men, two of whom wander here (lower left); in the south (upper right), much of the land is flat, lush, and tropical.

15

food and gifts, praised with hymns, and beseeched with supplications for rewards on earth and in the other world. Later, however, the fire sacrifice came to symbolize the cosmos, whose creation and maintenance, it was believed, depended upon the performance of this sacred ritual. Speculations on man and the universe eventually led Indian thinkers to complex, far-reaching views on the nature of ultimate reality. These speculations, combined with local, popular religious beliefs and aided by political and social changes, eventually coalesced in about 200 B.C. into a new religion—Hinduism.

Hinduism has no historic founder. It has no overall structured hierarchy of priests and, traditionally, no missionaries. It is a faith without a dogma, comprising three somewhat self-sufficient interrelated religions. Each is centered around the worship of a separate god (Vishnu, Devi, Shiva) and shares a common social system (caste) and many similar philosophical ideas. Within Hinduism's flexible and ambiguous borders are contained both highly abstract speculations about man and the universe and an intensely emotional devotion to a vast array of cosmic and nature deities. Hinduism honors its gods with elaborate rituals and organizes the lives of its adherents according to a complex set of social rules.

Most Indians are farmers who till the soil, tend their animals, and follow a traditional way of life. In this timeless scene—a familiar one throughout rural India—a goatherd drives his flock down a dusty village lane in Rajasthan.

17

Traditional Hindu Life

The center of Hindu life is the family. From birth to death, the life of a Hindu is circumscribed by familial responsibilities and the rituals of purification and worship that accompany them. Most Hindus live in a joint household, that is, all male members of a family along with their wives and children occupy one house (or group of houses), maintain a single kitchen, and own their land in common. The patriarch, or oldest male, is the head of the household, and he is treated with utmost respect by the rest of the family. His wife, and the other wives, aunts, and daughters, are usually occupied with housework and maintain a modest presence in the house. Children are treated with much love and respect. A Hindu woman especially longs to have a son to carry out life's rituals and perform the funeral rites that will insure the safe passage of her husband's soul from this world to the next. Elaborate ceremonies are undertaken to promote the conception of a child and to protect it while still in its mother's womb from spells cast by the evil eye or perhaps by a jealous relative, a barren or widowed sister-in-law, for example. The moment of birth brings great joy to the house, especially so if the child is a boy.

Members of a joint household—parents and children, grandparents, aunts, uncles, and cousins—gather in the courtyard of the house they share in Nasik, a city not far from Bombay. Traditionally, Hindu families live under one roof, cook in a common kitchen, and follow a complex set of religious rituals and social rules that define every aspect of their lives.

Surrounded by doting relatives and protected from evil influences by numerous rituals, a Hindu child grows up in a secure environment. Between the ages of eight and eleven a boy from one of the three higher classes will undergo an initiation rite, a "second birth," whereby he becomes a full member of his caste and of society. The ceremony includes two essential

19

features: the boy is granted the sacred thread (a cord of three twisted strands worn over the shoulder and across the chest), which from this day on he will wear continuously, and the first bit of sacred knowledge—a verse from the ancient Aryan sacred book, the Rig-Veda, known as the Gayatri—is whispered to him. According to religious texts, this initiation marks the first of the four stages of an ideal Hindu life—that of the student. During this period the boy remains celibate and spends his days studying religious texts with a teacher, or guru.

When he attains maturity, a Hindu must marry. More likely than not his marriage will be arranged by his family, and his wife will be chosen from the same caste. After many meetings between his family and that of his prospective bride, the consulting of horoscopes, and possibly the exchanging of a dowry, an agreement is struck and the date for the wedding is set. Donning elaborate ceremonial garb, he rides to the bride's house on a white horse at the head of a colorful and spirited procession, accompanied by musicians, torches, and images of the gods. The couple is married around a sacred fire amid the chants of priests, and then feasting, other ceremonies, and merrymaking follow, sometimes lasting for days. Marriage marks the beginning of the second stage of an ideal Hindu life—that of the householder—in

According to religious texts, an ideal Hindu life is divided into four stages, the first being that of the student. The foreheads, arms, shoulders, and chests of these South Indian students receiving religious instruction in Madras are marked with three colored streaks, which indicate that they are followers of the Hindu god Shiva. Their teacher (second from left) wears the sacred thread given to higher caste Hindus.

which a man settles down, raises a family, and tends to the duties of his caste and religion. This is the highest stage that most Hindus attain.

Daily life in a traditional Hindu home is quite similar throughout India. Members of the family are usually awake before sunrise. Since the first thing seen in the morning must be auspicious, a devout Hindu often keeps religious pictures or

Marriage marks the beginning of the second stage of an ideal Hindu life—that of the householder. Here, a veiled bride and a groom with a jeweled turban are seated before the sacred wedding fire. Their garments are tied together during the rites that seal their marriage.

objects near his bed. Upon rising, he rinses his mouth with water, cleanses his nasal passages and throat, and brushes his teeth with the twig of a tree (usually the bitter-barked neem tree). A daily bath in a river or pond, or in his house, follows. Besides cleansing the body, this bath is also believed to remove the harmful effects of the previous day's wrongdoings. To achieve this purification, the bather immerses himself in the water, sprinkles water over his

Hindu families maintain altars in their homes for daily ritual worship. This South Indian Brahman householder bows before images of the gods at his family altar, where garlands of flowers and offerings of food have been placed.

head with his right hand, pays homage to the sun, prays to diminish the effects of his wrongdoings, and makes offerings to the gods, the holy sages, and his ancestors.

Morning devotions, sacrifices, and other religious rituals usually follow the bath. Before breakfast, a devout Hindu might make an offering of clarified butter, curds, or other staples of the Indian diet to the fire that has cooked his meal; he might read religious texts or perform an act of pious charity. Most importantly, he will worship his special god either at home or in a temple. As with most aspects of traditional life, the sequence, number, and piety with which these rites are observed vary from person to person, but some or all of them are practiced by most Hindus. The purpose of these elaborate purifying rituals and religious ceremonies is to begin the day properly with the mind and body protected from evil, cleansed of physical and spiritual pollution, and centered upon life's important concerns.

Following these rituals, the morning meal is taken. Customarily, it consists of milk, flat breads, sweets, rice, and lentils, served on a tray or a leaf and eaten with the right hand. No utensils, except perhaps a spoon, are used. Meat is usually not eaten, since most Hindus are vegetarians. The remainder of the day is filled with the pursuit of an occupation broken by occasional cups of tea: for men, this frequently means plying a family trade passed on from father to son; for women, preparing meals, tending to children, and managing the household. At midday and twilight additional devotions may be observed. Dinner, normally consisting of vegetable dishes, lentils, curds, and rice or flat breads, is eaten later in the evening, about nine o'clock, after which the family retires for the night.

Life in a traditional Hindu family is defined by a number of ritual duties. One of the most important daily rites is bathing, regarded as an act of physical and spiritual cleansing. This pious Hindu, his hands folded in homage to the gods, performs his morning ablutions amid water lilies in a still pond.

Defined and circumscribed by duty and ritual, life in a traditional Hindu household assumes great regularity and serenity. Quietly it flows until death, when life begins again in another form. The death rites are among the most important and complex of Hindu rituals, and it is absolutely essential that they be performed correctly. When death draws near, a Hindu is moved from his bed to the ground, considered a more auspicious place to die. Soon after life departs, the body is wrapped in a cloth and carried on the shoulders of male relatives to the burning ground, which usually lies at the edge of a river. The body is first immersed in the river and then placed upon a wooden funeral pyre; the eldest son walks around it several times, sprinkles water on the body, and makes offerings of grains, clarified butter, and other basic substances. He then lights the pyre; after some hours, the corpse will have been consumed by the flames and the relatives then scatter the ashes on the river; what remains of the bones will be saved and taken later to another auspicious spot, where they will be cast into a river. Following the cremation, the dead person's family is considered ritually impure, a condition that only the passage of time and the performance of purification rites can alter. The most important rituals observed during this period are offerings the eldest son makes to the gods and to his ancestors to insure the safe and proper passage of the soul to the nether world and eventually to the point of rebirth.

27

Many years ago, women of certain castes chose to throw themselves onto their dead husbands' burning pyres rather than face the unhappy prospect of life without a spouse. Even today, long after this custom has ceased, a Hindu widow has little to look forward to, for usually she will not remarry, even if she is quite young, and must live out her life in the household of her dead husband.

A Hindu woman is not given a sacred thread in her childhood. Instead, she is brought up to assume the life-sustaining roles of wife and mother. As a girl, she learns domestic skills and takes part in rituals meant to ready her for her future. One of the most lovely rites is the No Salt Ceremony, observed in some Hindu families at the start of five consecutive monsoon seasons beginning when the girl is about seven. Each day, for five days in a row, a girl eats food that is not seasoned with salt, and worships tender seedlings sprouted from the barley and wheat seeds she planted before the festival. By participating in this and other rites, she is prepared for marriage and for childbearing. Until her wedding, a Hindu girl remains in her father's household; then she becomes part of her husband's joint family, and will stay there even after her husband's death although her presence may be regarded as inauspicious and a financial burden. To a traditional Hindu woman, her husband is a god, someone to be cared for, loved, and respected. As one sign of respect, a Hindu wife often walks a few steps behind her husband when they go out.

A woman's day begins, like that of a man, with a ritual bath. Marketing and preparing meals, mending clothes, tending children, dealing with the tensions that arise in a large joint family, and participating in Hindu rituals usually fill the rest of the day. Occasionally, fasts and rituals specifically associated with marriage and childbirth break up this routine. Although she may seem to be placed in a subordinate position, a Hindu woman assumes her role in the nurturing and sustaining of human life with seriousness and dignity. She is, accordingly, treated with great respect.

Cooking, caring for children, and observing religious rituals fill the days of most Hindu women. Their traditional role as wives and mothers, nurturing and sustaining human life, affords them a position of great respect.

Initiation, marriage, maintenance of a family, and fulfillment of social and religious obligations mark the turning points of life for most Hindus. However, for a few, the pursuit of something more beckons, and Hindu tradition assigns to these people two stages beyond those of student and householder. The third is that of the forest dweller, a man who, retiring from the life of a householder, lives along with his wife as a recluse dedicating himself to religious pursuits. The fourth and final stage is that of a begging wanderer (sannyasi), who, abandoning all ties with this world, wanders homeless in search of ultimate Truth.

A sannyasi spends his time in meditation and pilgrimage to sacred spots. He begs for his food and eats only enough to sustain life. Everything that he once had is cast away—his possessions, his wife, his family, and his caste. Should he meet his wife or his brother after his renunciation, he will stare blankly at them though they might weep or call out his name, for they now mean nothing to him. All bonds of emotion, longing, and love have been extinguished. To the world around him, the sannyasi is a dead man; he has passed beyond its good and evil, love and hate, likes and dislikes, and continually dwells at the threshold of the boundless. Although forest dwellers are not usually encountered,

For those who wish to realize fully the greater reality that lies beyond the everyday world of marriage and family, Hinduism offers two additional stages of the ideal life, those of the forest dweller and the homeless mendicant, one of whom is seen here carrying a covered staff over his shoulder and trudging up the sandy banks of the Ganges in Benares.

for this stage is rarely followed by Hindus today, wandering mendicants can be seen throughout the length and breadth of India, in city streets and village lanes, high in the Himalayas—everywhere, and yet nowhere, for they pass like shadows from one place to another, from the physical world to that which lies beyond.

What is it that these homeless sannyasis seek in their eternal wandering? What is it that the householder hopes for in his faithful adherence to his duties and the student prepares his mind to receive? What is it that every Hindu ultimately searches for? Hindu religious texts teach that life has four basic aims. The first is dharma, the pursuit of law, human righteousness, duty, and cosmic order; the second, artha, the accumulation of worldly success; and the third, kama, the pursuit of love. But it is the fourth, moksha, or release, that is the most important. Release from what? Release from the empty pleasures and unavoidable pain of life in the everyday world, so that one might fully realize and merge with the Absolute. All Hindu life is focused upon this, the ultimate aim and purpose of existence.

Although life as a holy man is traditionally assigned to the later years, some people, such as this young follower of the Hindu god Vishnu, decide to pursue a religious life at an early age. The matted hair of the youth is tied in an ascetic's topknot; the trident, an attribute sacred to the Hindu god Shiva, rests against a wall behind him.

Existence and Release

Daybreak on the seacoast of Orissa. Hindus believe that the everyday world—bounded by sunrise and sunset, birth and death—and the individual lives of all beings within it pass through endless cycles of death and rebirth. The ultimate aim of Hindu life is to attain release from this world and to merge with the eternal, boundless Absolute.

In India the Absolute is conceived of in many different ways. Almost all schools of Hindu religious and philosophical thought believe, however, that some absolute reality underlies and permeates the everyday world in which we live. The Absolute is usually thought to be supremely real: it is without parts or divisions, without beginning or end. It is One. Daily life, on the other hand, is believed to be ultimately unreal or, even if real, to be something that clouds our vision of the Absolute. In complete contrast to the perfect and undivided Absolute, the everyday world teems with impermanent and imperfect forms of life, with people belonging to the four great classes, with animals and flowers, with trees and birds. Its borders are birth and death. It is the world that we see around us.

According to Hindu beliefs, the universe passes through endlessly repeating cycles of creation and destruction. It is born from the cosmic ocean, continues on for aeons, and then it is utterly destroyed by fire at the end of a cosmic era. After some time, the entire creative-destructive process begins anew and the universe is born only to die once more. Each cosmic era, from its watery beginning to its fiery end, is divided into four ages, the first being superior, and the others showing a progressive decline in morality, vitality, and happiness. Disintegration, rather than progress, marks the passage of time.

Paralleling the notion of cycles of evolution and time is the Hindu belief that a man lives more than one life, that is, he is born, dies, and is reborn again in another form. If in a past time he has led a virtuous life, he will be reborn into a higher plane of existence, for it is the full effect of actions, or karma, in this life that determines one's character and form—animal, human, demonic, or divine—in the next. The law of karma is inescapable: every good or evil deed will eventually bear its fruit, either in this existence or a later one. Life, then, becomes a continuous passage of the soul from one body and level of existence to another, a passage that is often visualized as a perpetually turning wheel.

Man's ultimate folly lies in believing that this ever-changing and fleeting universe, filled with diverse forms of being, is permanent and real. Foolishly desiring the pleasures of everyday life, he dedicates his entire being to pursuing them. But in so doing, he identifies himself only further with it and thus more thoroughly entraps and enmeshes himself in its endless cycles of birth and death, pain and pleasure. To escape the terrible fate of dying again and again, man must realize that his true self is not identical with his body and its desires. He must break out of his bondage to daily existence and turn his attention toward the Absolute. It is only through complete identification, absorption, and integration with the Absolute that man can be released from the illusory, everyday world and from its cycles of endless death and rebirth.

How can release be attained? For many Hindus, the path to release lies in action and duty. Their goal is to do good works without concern for reward, observe faithfully the duties of class and caste, worship the gods, support holy men, and perform prescribed rituals. In so doing, they hope to be reborn in increasingly higher states following a path that, however slowly, might lead to release.

Hindus believe that knowledge gained through yogic meditation and discipline offers one path to release. This aged holy man, seated in a yogic posture, recites mantras on the bank of the river Ganges in Benares.

A second path, and therefore another source of hope, is also possible. This is the path of intense love for a personal god. By truly loving him, by seeking refuge in him, by completely surrendering to him, the devotee hopes that the gracious deity will grant release from death and rebirth and offer integration with the Absolute. For a Hindu whose lowly social position denies access to certain religious rituals, and guarantees that almost endless rebirth would be required to attain release through proper living, the way of love gives hope.

Yet another path exists, one that offers hope for release in the present lifetime. This is the route usually taken only by sannyasis and other holy men, the difficult path of knowledge and yogic meditation. Through yoga, a system of spiritual and physical exercises meant to still the mind, one may attain union with the Absolute, be it conceived as an abstraction or as embodied in a

Ritual worship of the gods and faithful observation of caste rules and family responsibilities are also a path to release. In a narrow lane in Benares, filled with tea stands and shops, this husband and wife stop to pay homage to images of the gods housed in a small shrine: with their reverent hand gesture, they greet and respectfully honor the deity.

Intense love for a personal deity—reflected on the rapt faces of South Indian women in Madras—offers another path to release. By adoring and completely surrendering to a god, his followers hope that he will grant them release from the endless cycles of death and rebirth.

deity. Yogic exercises involve controlled posture, breathing, and diet, and abstention from sexual activity. The purpose of this experience is to negate disturbances from the senses or the external world, so that the yogi's mind can focus totally upon the Absolute—the object of his meditation. Then, often with the aid of pictures and diagrams that depict a specific embodiment of the ultimate reality, he is able to concentrate his mind so fully that he feels no difference between himself and the Absolute. By thus identifying with ultimate reality, by realizing that his true self is one with it, and by merging with it, the yogi attains release, that which lies at the end of the cycles of existence, thereby escaping rebirth.

Although each of these paths is a distinct channel to release, the practice of one by no means excludes the others. A Hindu may, for instance, obey his caste and class obligations and worship the gods, thereby following the path of duty, and at the same time experience an intense, spontaneous love for a deity and hope for salvation through an act of grace.

In Hinduism, there are three major and equally important gods, or embodiments of the Absolute—Vishnu, Devi, and Shiva—each of whom is the center of a separate devotional cult. A devout Hindu usually worships one of the three as the supreme god, who creates, maintains, and destroys the universe, and regards the other two major gods as secondary aspects of him. The selection of one of the three deities as a personal god is largely an individual decision: within a family, for instance, the mother may be a follower of the Great Goddess, Devi; her son, a devotee of Shiva; and her husband's family all ardent worshipers of Vishnu in his form as the beloved Krishna. In addition to worshiping a supreme god, a Hindu will also honor a local family deity as well as a number of the thousands of minor Hindu gods and spirits whose presence, indicated by a daub of color, a flag, an earthen pot, or some other simple sign, can be felt at all times in India.

Although they share many of the same traits, each of the three supreme gods has an individual nature. Vishnu, the Pervader, is a kind, adaptable god who works continuously for the world's welfare. In the Aryan sacred texts, the Vedas, Vishnu was a deity

Hinduism recognizes three supreme gods or specific embodiments of the Absolute—Vishnu, Devi, and Shiva. Vishnu is a benevolent god who protects the universe from evil and preserves cosmic order. He is depicted here in a carved stone image from Deogarh (sixth century), sleeping on the cosmic serpent in the interval between the destruction of one world and the creation of the next: Hindus believe that the cosmos undergoes endless cycles of death and rebirth.

associated with the sun. Later, however, the interweaving of Vishnu with other gods, culture heroes, and animal spirits helped to give him a broader, more universal meaning. This process of assimilation was made easier by the belief in the avatars—descents or incarnations—of Vishnu: it is said that whenever the universe is in danger of total destruction at the hands of an evil demon, Vishnu assumes a bodily form and descends to this world to save it. Traditionally, ten avatars of Vishnu are reckoned: Fish, Tortoise, Boar, Man-Lion, Dwarf, Rama with a Battle-Ax, Rama, Krishna, Buddha, and Kalkin (The One on a White Horse), the incarnation yet to come. Krishna and Rama are both very immediate, vital forms of Vishnu whose cares and actions fall well within the realm of normal human understanding. They are particularly popular in modern India and have independent cults of their own.

Devi, the Great Goddess, has probably been worshiped in one form or another in India since the time of the Indus Valley culture, and perhaps even earlier. She has an ambiguous nature and appears in many forms. In her benevolent aspects she is the Great Mother, a goddess of abundance, fertility, and childbirth; in her terrific, or destructive, forms, she is the valiant demon-fighter Durga and the bloodthirsty, all-destroying Kali. The goddess's devotees regard her as the embodiment of universal energy: she is believed to be the potency that dwells in each of the male gods, and the spark that arouses them to action. Devi enjoys wide devotion all over India, but she has a particularly large following in eastern India in the state of West Bengal.

Shiva is the third supreme Hindu god. This many-faceted deity evolved from an amalgamation of the Aryan god Rudra, the Great Archer, and bestower of healing herbs, and various indigenous gods of fertility and potency. Unlike the benevolent Vishnu, Shiva belongs to the night, the moon, and to all that is dark and mysterious. He is one of the most complex divinities known to man.

Like Vishnu and Shiva, the Great Goddess Devi, regarded as an embodiment of the Absolute, appears in many forms. This opulent image, made for the festival of Durgapuja ("Worship of Durga"), depicts her as the demon-killer Durga. Majestically riding her rearing animal mount (lower left), she effortlessly pierces the green demon Mahisha (lower right) with the end of a trident, one of her many weapons.

Shiva,
Lord
of
Existence

Who is Shiva? What is Shiva? To his devotees, Shiva is everything: he is the root and support of the universe; he is the creative-destructive flow of life that rushes through it. He is motion and calm, male and female, light and dark, ascetic and lover, everything and its opposite. Shiva is an ambiguous god who embodies, defines, and reconciles within himself all of life's processes and paradoxes. Shiva is existence. He embodies the structure of the whole universe; he is also its potent, all-pervasive energy—a radiant force that appears in many forms (light, fire, the heat of sexual passion, ascetic discipline), which he uses to create, maintain, and destroy, and to release every being in the universe.

In his absolute state, Shiva is limitless and unfettered, exceeding all definition. He exists in this state as an undivided whole that lies beyond gender, measure, and form. When he desires to reveal himself to his devotees, Shiva leaves his eternal, formless state and enters into an intermediate state in which his essence is said to exist, but not in a particular visible shape. Leaving this intermediary state, Shiva finally appears in numerous, visible, paradoxical forms to his devotees, who live in the concrete world of measure, time, and activity.

Shiva is called in sacred texts by countless names. Some, such as the Three-Eyed One and the Blue-Throated One, describe his forms or attributes; others, such as Destroyer of the Three Cities and Lord of the Dance, refer to his mythical activities. Still other names, such as the Immovable, the Terrible, and the Abode of

To his followers, Shiva is Lord of Existence: he embodies the structure and energy of the entire universe, he reconciles within himself all of life's processes and paradoxes. This complex image, carved in a cave temple on the island of Elephanta near Bombay (sixth century), is one of the most profoundly moving images of Shiva ever created.

45

Bliss, refer to his ascetic, terrific, or kindly aspects. Each of his names reveals one facet of Shiva's complex personality, but none expresses all of it.

Why does Shiva appear in so many different forms? Why is he called by so many names? It is because he is existence; and existence, according to Hindu thought, includes not only the countless forms, complexities, and polarities of the everyday world, but also the solitary, undivided Absolute that underlies and permeates them. Shiva, being a god who is, embodies, and mirrors all of existence, therefore, possesses countless visible forms as well as a single, nonmanifest Absolute one. To be Lord of Existence, he must contain, reconcile, and dominate all aspects of it.

Shiva reveals himself in many different and often contradictory forms, one of the most important being Lord of the Dance—depicted here in a bronze figure from South India (tenth century). Shiva's dance symbolizes the cosmic energy that he embodies and directs toward creating, sustaining, and destroying the universe. From the sound of the drum held in his upper right hand, creation arises; with a lick of the flame in his upper left, the universe is destroyed. Shiva tramples the demon of ignorant forgetfulness, for through his creative-destructive dance he reminds his devotees that belief in the reality and permanence of the fleeting everyday world is foolish. It is through the revelation of this truth that he offers hope for release. (Los Angeles County Museum of Art, Anonymous Gift)

The energy that Shiva embodies is often used to destroy evil forces and demons as he does in this image (left) of Shiva as the Destroyer of Time from a temple wall in Pattadakal (seventh–eighth century). According to myth, Shiva saved the pious sixteen-year-old Markandeya by first overpowering the God of Death (and, hence, Time) and then granting the boy eternal life.

As the embodiment of procreative energy, Shiva is a husband and father. In this charming and, perhaps, deceptively calm painting (right) from the Punjab Hills (early nineteenth century), a five-faced Shiva and his family ride their mounts through the countryside after having descended from Kailasa, the Himalayan home of the Great God. Shiva sits on the bull Nandi; Parvati, his wife, on a lion; his elephant-headed son Ganesha, on a rat; and his six-faced son Karttikeya, on a peacock. (Private collection, on loan to the Museum Rietberg, Zurich)

The varied forms in which Shiva appears in the constantly changing, everyday world are often contradictory. Believed by his devotees to be the embodiment of procreative energy, Shiva is thus said to be a great lover, husband of the goddess Parvati, father of the six-faced god Karttikeya and the elephant-headed god Ganesha, and the creator of the universe. At the same time, however, Shiva is a destroyer who uses his energy to annihilate the world at the end of time. If in one of his aspects Shiva is a married householder, in another he is an unmarried ascetic who,

49

through yogic exercises and continence, channels his energy toward realizing the Absolute. In so doing, Shiva shows man how to attain release from the illusory world that he, as its creator, has made. Shiva is able to assume so many contradictory forms because the cosmic energy that he embodies pervades the universe and can be directed toward any end. In his many forms, Shiva encompasses every aspect of life as it is conceived by Hindus.

To understand even a part of Shiva's nature and to worship him is to perceive and participate in the mystery of existence. To make contact with Shiva is to come in touch with a deity of immense power. Shiva is not regarded by his devotees with the joy offered to Krishna or the admiration showered upon the noble Rama. Rather, he is viewed with respect, and perhaps fear, for Shiva is the Great God, praised for his awesome powers and his amazing feats of asceticism, and feared for his sudden fits of seeming madness. Devotees come to Shiva for many different reasons. Some approach him in times of trouble or sickness; some wish only to adore him; and others come to identify with him so fully that they lose their individuality and attain liberation.

While in one of his aspects Shiva is a conventional, married householder, in others he is a solitary ascetic, a frequenter of foul-smelling cremation grounds, and a companion of blood-crazed ghouls. In this painting from the Punjab Hills (late eighteenth century), the Great God beats a drum and dances with the hideous Kali—a destructive aspect of the goddess Devi—accompanied by animals who play musical instruments. Their music excites other demons, who, brandishing swords and bowls made from skulls, dance across the hills beyond. (Collection Dr. and Mrs. Oscar Leneman)

Ways
to
Shiva

Ritual worship of the linga—the chief symbol of Shiva—is a complex and moving ceremony, conducted here by priests at the golden Vishvanatha Temple in Benares. By evoking Shiva's presence in the linga and honoring it with baths, flowers, and entertainment, devotees hope that the Great God will shower benefits upon the whole community. Here the ceremony is nearly finished. The linga, now fully covered with flowers and serpent ornaments, rests in its silver tank; at the center, a priest lights small lamps while others hold bells and lamps used to entertain the god. Devotees, present more as an audience than as a congregation, quietly watch from the sanctuary's door.

In order to meditate upon, worship, and identify with Shiva, one must make contact with him. Most Hindus come in touch with Shiva by using rituals to evoke his presence. While to some extent they are used by those following the ways of love and knowledge, rituals are especially important to those who pursue the path of action and duty in hopes of attaining release in some future existence.

The basic ritual means used to make contact with Shiva are mantras, yantras, mudras, and images. A mantra is a sound or group of sounds recited, often almost endlessly, to call up an aspect of a deity. When a devotee utters a certain mantra, he is able to evoke one form of Shiva in his mind for worship. He may also approach Shiva by meditating upon a Shiva yantra, an abstract geometrical figure that captures an aspect of the god and diagrams his basic energies. Through the yantra, the vision and inner presence of Shiva are brought to the mind of the devotee. Each portion of the yantra has significance for the devotee; as a whole, the diagram reveals the inner meaning of the aspect of Shiva that it depicts. Mudras are specific ritual hand gestures often made while saying a mantra or meditating upon a yantra that help to establish more firmly the bond between the devotee and Shiva.

Communication with Shiva may also be made by seeing and touching his various symbols and images, thereby drawing the Great God close to the worshiper. By ritually touching the parts of the image with his gaze, and then touching with his hands the

Temples of Shiva are considered the residences of the Great God on earth. Housing images and symbols of Shiva, they are regarded as places where a devotee may make special contact with the god. The Arunacaleshvara Temple in Tiruvannamalai (seventeenth century), typical of those of South India, consists of a darkened central shrine and many pillared halls, surrounded by several walls pierced by enormous, elaborately decorated gateways.

same parts of his own body, the devotee effects a magic transfer of his "living self," thereby becoming one with the deity. Although the image represents Shiva, it is not identical with him. Rather, it is a concrete form in which Shiva resides when he appears in the everyday world. Before the ritual of consecration, known as the "Eye Opening Ceremony," an image is regarded only as a work of art. Even afterward, if the rituals evoking Shiva's presence are not continuously performed, the image loses its power because the god does not inhabit it. Only if properly and respectfully invited will Shiva come to reside in his images, and thus graciously offer a vision of himself to the devotee.

54

The plan of the Vishvanatha Temple (above) in Khajuraho in northern India (eleventh century), like that of other Shiva temples, follows a sacred geometric diagram that reflects the movements of the heavenly bodies. The main sanctuary of the Kandariya Mahadeo Temple (right) in Khajuraho (eleventh century), lying deep inside the temple, is roofed by the soaring spire at the rear; the smaller spires cover various pillared halls leading from the temple's entrance at the right.

Images of Shiva may be seen almost everywhere in India, in household shrines, shops, and on the streets; but most importantly, they are a part of temples dedicated to the Great God. However large or small, each temple of Shiva is regarded as his residence in this world and the place in which he appears to his devotees. It is a place of passage between the everyday world and the Absolute. At a temple, prayers are more easily heard and readily granted because contact with Shiva is more direct and immediate. People visit the temple to identify with and to

meditate upon the Great God, to seek his help in solving human problems (desire for male offspring, financial success, and the like), or to honor a vow made to him. The temple is an auspicious place because it houses powerful images that the worshiper believes will assist him in communicating with Shiva.

The most important part of a Shiva temple is a relatively small, dark cell called the "womb chamber." It houses the temple's main object of worship—the linga, a symbol of the god. A very tall, elaborately carved spire rises directly above it, and several halls, some capped by smaller spires, are placed along an axis in front of its main door. The outside walls of the temple are embellished with carved images: the lower parts include figures of gods, men, plants, and animals; the upper parts are usually decorated with more abstract patterns.

Devotees perform ritual ablutions in the bathing tank of the Shri Nataraja Temple in Chidambaram. Bathing in such sacred tanks at specific times is believed to bring special benefits to devotees.

Often smaller shrines to lesser, or local, gods and several separate pillared halls are located on the temple grounds. Sometimes an old bilva (wood apple) tree, which is sacred to Shiva, or a banyan tree grows near the temple; around the lower part of its gnarled trunk may be a platform or altar upon which various small images of the gods are placed. In most temples, too, a bathing tank is located close to the sanctuary: usually it is rectangular with stone steps on each side leading down to the sacred and potent waters. If in smaller temples, or those in congested urban areas, a bathing tank or a stream does not exist, a well will be dug, or merely a pot of water provided. The presence of water is absolutely necessary for ceremonial purification and for use in the various temple rituals.

When a devotee goes to a Shiva temple, or to that of any other god, he will usually present floral offerings purchased from vendors such as these at the great temple in Madura.

The temple grounds are often surrounded by a wall that separates the sacred area from the everyday world. Close by this wall, or somewhere else within the temple compound, are the living quarters of the Brahman priest who performs the temple's rites. Outside, somewhere near the wall, are the open stalls of merchants who sell religious souvenirs, garlands of brightly

Two devotees, one with her hands joyfully clasped in homage, pass under a painted, carved relief of Shiva signaling a gateway to the great temple in Madura. A seated vendor sells garlands of flowers for offerings to the god.

Vendors of painted plaster statues of gods are a common sight near temples and pilgrimage centers, and on city streets at the time of religious festivals. These images are purchased by devotees to be taken home and honored as sacred souvenirs.

colored flowers, coconuts, and other items that worshipers purchase to bring as offerings to the god. Even in the bustle of this market, religious considerations have their place: one must never, for instance, smell the flower garlands because their fragrance is meant only for Shiva; if one does, they become contaminated and the vendor may not in good faith sell the flowers.

The main object of worship in a Shiva temple (above) is the linga—the sign or symbol of Shiva. Placed in the inner sanctuary, the linga , such as this one in a temple in Aihole (seventh–ninth century), marks Shiva's presence and represents him as the Axis of Existence and the source of universal energy.

According to legend, Shiva appeared as a fiery linga pillar (right) when Vishnu and Brahma each claimed to have created the universe. Vishnu in his boar form dove into the deep to discover the linga's base; Brahma in his goose form flew up to find its top. After both had failed, Shiva revealed himself as the creator of the universe. In this painting from Jodhpur (mid-nineteenth century), Shiva is shown in the linga of flames. Respectfully bowing before him are Brahma (left) and Vishnu (right); Devi sits at right. (Collection William Theo Brown and Paul Wonner)

The general placement of the images of a Shiva temple is strictly governed by sacred texts. The temple's main object of worship—the linga—placed within the womb chamber, is the sign of the Great God: it marks his presence in that spot. Symbolically, it represents Shiva as the energy and support of existence, as the god in whom every cosmic process begins and ends. It is the most abstract, complex, and comprehensive symbol associated with the Great God.

Although lingas can be formed from almost any substance— earth, metal, sand, rice, cow dung, flowers—those housed in temples are usually made of large, heavy, vertical stones. Some of these lingas are "self born": stones found in their natural state and believed to have come into existence by themselves when time began; others are carefully carved by artists into pillarlike shafts with curved tops. Stark and geometric, the linga is meant to represent, in an abstract fashion, an erect phallus and a pillar. As a pillar, it stands for Shiva as the Axis of Existence, which Hindus

believe extends from the Absolute to the everyday world. From this axis, the world is born, and it is to this axis that it will return before complete annihilation at the end of time.

As an erect phallus, excited and full of potentiality, the linga is a fitting expression of Shiva as the embodiment of all the energy in existence. The Great God often channels his energy toward sets of contradictory ends. On the one hand, the linga expresses the energy used by the Great God to create the world, for it can be thought to represent the phallus at the moment of the seed's release. On the other hand, the linga also expresses the energy used to transcend the everyday world, for it is thought to represent the erect phallus of Shiva, the yogi, who instead of expending this energy by release, retains his seed and directs his power, under the control of ascetic discipline, toward enlightenment and integration with the Absolute. Shiva, as Lord of Yogis, is the chief practitioner and teacher of this means of release. Shiva is a life-giving creator as well as a life-transcending ascetic because the energy that he embodies (and which is symbolized by the linga) can be directed toward any end.

Located at the center of the temple's womb chamber, the linga serves as the point upon which various images of Shiva are architecturally positioned: in most Shiva temples these images are placed in elaborate niches that rest at the center of each of the walls of the womb chamber. They derive their sacred potency from the energy that "radiates" from the linga, and they give fuller exposition to its complex meaning. Most of these images show Shiva in one of his many human forms, as creator, destroyer, ascetic. Or they may depict his wife Parvati and his sons Ganesha and Karttikeya, all of whom are extensions of his divine power.

Shiva is portrayed in this sculptured relief (ninth century) from a temple in Tamil Nadu as a protective, loving husband affectionately embracing his wife Parvati.

Various images of Shiva in human form are also placed on other walls of the temple. One such image depicts Shiva as a dancer. The rhythmic movement of his dance is an image of the cosmic energy that Shiva, as Lord of Existence, embodies. Like the linga, the dance is a concentration of heightened energy that may explode in any one of a variety of movements and gestures. Shiva performs many dances. In some, he dances—that is, he

Shiva is the totality of existence—male and female, light and dark, creation and destruction. One of his many forms is that of Shiva, the Lord Whose Half Is Woman, shown here in a relief from a temple in Orissa (ninth century). His right half depicts Shiva as a male; he holds a trident attribute in his upper right hand; the other right hand points down to the bull Nandi. The left half of the god shows Shiva as a female, holding a mirror and touching the head of the lion mount sacred to the goddess Parvati.

channels his energy—to create the world, to sustain its rhythmic life, and to destroy it; in others, however, he directs his energy toward more limited ends.

The appearance of all representations of Shiva is carefully regulated by a canon of proportions and codified postures, gestures, and attributes. The figure's imposing presence, many arms, and breath-inflated body tell the devotee that it is a representation of a god; his hair, tied up in the ascetic's topknot, and attributes such as the trident that he bears in one of his hands and a third eye on his forehead, immediately identify the figure as Shiva, for these features are common to most of his human representations. The attributes held in Shiva's other hands—the fire of destruction or a drum from whose sound creation arises, for example—reveal his various powers and energies and help to define his identity. Shiva needs multiple arms to display simultaneously his many attributes, and to remind the devotee that even though assuming human form, he differs from and is infinitely more powerful than ordinary mortals.

Outside and directly in front of the womb chamber lies an image of a reclining bull, Nandi, positioned so that he gazes through the womb chamber's doorway at the linga housed within. Nandi is Shiva in his animal form. From one point of view, the sexually potent bull is an expression of Shiva's cosmic energy directed toward the creation of the universe. And yet, at the same time, he symbolizes the use of Shiva's energy toward spiritual ends, for Nandi is also the mount that the Great God rides. Nandi's bestial instincts are thus kept in rein by the Great God, just as Shiva, with his yogic discipline, retains his seed and directs his energy toward release from the world. Thus tamed, Nandi is Shiva's greatest devotee. Indeed, the name "Nandi" means bliss, and lying directly in front of the linga, gazing at it with affection, Nandi lives in a state of perpetual adoration.

The temple's images are reverenced with elaborate ceremonies collectively known as temple puja, or worship, that are performed by a Brahman priest twice a day (at sunrise and sunset), three times (at sunrise, noon, and sunset), or four (at sunrise, noon, sunset, and midnight), depending upon the size and wealth of the temple. The image is treated much like a maharaja or an honored guest: it is washed, perfumed, clothed, garlanded, fed, and entertained. The purpose of such respectful attention is to evoke Shiva's presence in the image and then to honor him properly in hopes of gaining his favors and of identifying with him.

Certain elements and a basic sequence of steps are included in most temple worship ceremonies. Before sunrise Shiva is awakened with the sound of drums, bells, and the blowing of a conch shell. The priest bathes himself, performs his regular morning rites, and cleanses the temple's womb chamber. When the time for the morning worship arrives, the priest appears, bare chested, wearing a sacred thread and a dhoti, a broad cloth that is first wrapped around the lower half of his body, then pulled between

Wherever a linga exists, an image of Nandi, the bull, will usually lie contentedly before it. Nandi is the god Shiva himself as well as, paradoxically, his animal mount and his most ardent devotee. At right, two Nandis gaze with complete adoration at the lingas (not seen) housed in shrines off a cloistered hall at the Brihadeshvara Temple in Tanjore.

Also from South India is this beautifully ornamented stone image of Nandi (twelfth century). (Philadelphia Museum of Art)

Devotees of Shiva usually have a deep affection for Nandi. In Shiva temples, Nandi is often reverenced with baths, incense, and flowers just before worship of the Shiva linga. The temple priest (left) tenderly decorates an image of the bull. Ceremonial objects used for the worship of Shiva (right) are respectfully arranged at the base of a huge stone linga in the Hazareshwar Temple in Udaipur, Rajasthan. At right is a lighted, five-wicked oil lamp and in front, a handbell, both used to entertain the god. A camphor holder rests at front, and behind it are burning incense sticks. At left is a mirror held up to the linga so that Shiva may see himself.

his legs and tucked in at the back of his waist. In larger temples, or in smaller ones at festival times, assistants may help in performing the rites; usually, however, only one assistant is necessary.

The priest begins the morning worship by honoring the images of the divinities on the temple's outer walls. He usually begins with the elephant-headed god Ganesha, the lord who both creates and removes obstacles. Washing or sprinkling the image with sacred water, the priest chants mantras that evoke the god's presence in his image and asks him to receive the gifts offered. He then marks the forehead of the image with fragrant sandalwood paste and decorates it with flower garlands, and may also make offerings of food or scented colored powders. Next, the images of Nandi, Parvati, and the goddess of the Ganges, as well as the metal vessels, lamps, and other objects to be used in the ritual, are also honored in much the same manner.

The linga of Shiva is worshiped with rituals such as this one being performed at the golden Vishvanatha Temple in Benares. The purpose of this ceremony is to evoke Shiva's presence in the linga and to honor it in hopes of receiving favors from the Great God. One of the Brahman priests begins the worship ceremony by bathing the black stone linga, which lies at the center of a silver tank, with water poured from a ritual vessel (left). Next, the priests wash the linga in the Five Ambrosias—milk, curds, clarified butter, sugar, and honey, and then (right) they cleanse it again with water.

Having thus worshiped the attendant gods and goddesses, the priest now begins to reverence the temple's main object of worship—the linga. Entering the womb chamber, he sits on the ground, performs yogic breathing exercises, and announces his intention to worship Shiva in the form of a linga. After saying the various mantras and making the mudras necessary to install various gods in different parts of his body, the priest utters an incantation to rid the area of evil spirits. Then, fixing his mind and meditating upon the linga, he begins by bathing it with water poured from a brass or copper pot. Next, he pours milk, curds, clarified butter, honey, and sugar (the Five Ambrosias) over the linga. Again, the linga is washed, and then it is marked all around with three lines of sandalwood paste. Rice is washed and placed on the linga, and it is decorated with garlands of flowers, scented colored powders, and if the temple is wealthy, rich bejeweled ornaments made of silver or gold. Having been bathed with costly offerings, scented, and adorned, the god residing in the linga may be fanned with fly whisks, while sometimes a mirror is placed before him so that he may see himself. When all this is completed, the priest rings a small handbell and censes the image with aromatic camphor; he sets uncooked food, fruits, and spices

before it as an offering. Finally, the resplendent and fully prepared linga is entertained: the priest waves a five-wicked oil lamp several times before the linga, while ringing the handbell and chanting mantras. Amid the sound of bells, the fragrance of incense, and the brilliance of vividly colored flowers, devotees bow their heads; some prostrate themselves before the image in which Shiva is fully present, for this is the moment of complete surrender and union. The god has come. He is in this place.

Temple puja is not truly congregational worship, but devotees do attend the ceremony as an audience. Some are present only for a short time: they reverently present their offerings to a priest who receives them on Shiva's behalf. They behold the image of the god, make their requests to him, say mantras, and then leave. Others, however, will sit or stand throughout the ceremony, praying and singing devotional songs at appropriate times.

When the worship has ended, the priest places his lighted lamp at the doorstep of the womb chamber. The devotees stretch out their hands toward the flame and then quickly touch their eyes in an act of homage and identification. Oftentimes, too, when the ceremony is over, the worshipers will perform a ritual walk around the temple. In so doing they will not cross the channel in

the ground that drains away the water that was poured over the linga, for this water is believed to be both sacred and somewhat dangerous. Consequently, they begin to walk around the shrine clockwise, with their right shoulders toward the linga. When they reach the channel, however, they retrace their path back to the starting place at the statue of Nandi, and then begin their circumambulation again. This time, with their left shoulders toward the shrine, they move in a counter-clockwise direction until reaching the water channel.

The noon, evening, and nighttime temple worship ceremonies are similar to the one held in the morning, but with some variations. For instance, the midday worship usually includes offerings of cooked food that are set before the linga on a ground purified by rituals; and the late-night puja in some temples ends with the priest draping a cloth over the linga so that the god will

During the worship of the linga in the Vishvanatha Temple in Benares, priests mark the linga with fragrant sandalwood paste (above left), and then place garlands of flowers on it (above right). Next, the linga is adorned with silver serpent ornaments and garlanded with more flowers (opposite left). Having been bathed, scented, ornamented, and garlanded, the linga is then entertained (opposite right) with the waving of lighted, five-wicked oil lamps, the ringing of hand-bells, and the chanting of mantras and verses. This moment is the culmination of the ceremony.

be warm when he sleeps. Since Shiva is an ascetic, the various pujas offered to him are actually rather simple: those given to Vishnu, who is regarded by his followers primarily as a king, are often much more elaborate.

Throughout the day, regardless of whether worship ceremonies are being performed or not, devotees, with their speech, bodies, and minds centered on Shiva, come to honor and make contact with him. Upon entering the temple, they summon the attention of the god by ringing a bell hanging near the womb chamber; after touching Nandi's head, they make offerings of flowers or food to the linga, or pour water upon it, and then, muttering prayers and mantras, bow or prostrate themselves before it. Devotees may also perform other pious acts at a temple; sometimes they pay a priest to repeat the names of Shiva for them or to have the linga bathed with water or the Five Ambrosias. Often, too, devotees will purify themselves by taking a bath in the sacred tank or a river that lies close by the temple.

People also visit a temple to be refreshed by its sacred atmosphere. In its courtyards and open halls, some listen to the discourses of holy men or to readings of sacred texts; others say Shiva mantras or repeat the names of Shiva, while counting them on rosaries (strings of beads made from dried berries), or sing devotional songs. The temple is a sacred spot, close to Shiva and

to all the gods. Despite the constant flow of devotees, it is a place of great stillness and intense emotion, for no matter how many people are there, the temple is a place where each follower of Shiva stands alone before his god.

Temples frequently serve as a focus for the celebration of special days and festivals honoring Shiva. Perhaps the most important Shiva festival is the Mahashivaratri (The Great Night of Shiva), which honors the night Shiva appeared to the gods Brahma and Vishnu as a flaming pillar of fire in order to demonstrate his supremacy over all the gods. It also commemorates, in some regions of India, the wedding of Shiva and Parvati. This festival is celebrated with fasting, a nightlong vigil, and worship of the linga in Shiva temples. Every Monday throughout the year is also sacred to Shiva and his devotees will always try to go to his temples on that day; the four summer Mondays of the Indian month of Shravan are especially holy, and fasts, visits to temples, and special pujas are undertaken.

A visit to any temple is a pilgrimage. Some sacred sites are considered more important than others, however, and a journey to them is longed for by most Hindus. Usually located on the tops of prominent mountains or on riverbanks, sources, confluences, or by the sea—that is, at places of passage, meeting, or transition—these holy spots are associated through various myths with specific deities. Hindus believe that a pilgrimage to these special sites and the performance of certain rites there will yield benefits in this world and, perhaps, a better existence in the next. A pilgrimage is often made to enlist the aid of a god in solving a problem or to honor a vow made to him. These sites are also auspicious spots for consigning the remains of the dead to the waters and for performing ceremonies for the deceased and purifying rituals for a bride-to-be. The time for making a

pilgrimage must be auspicious; and the fasting and self-restraint that usually precede the journey, as well as the hardships encountered along the way, help to discipline and purify the pilgrim. During a pilgrimage, the devotee will usually worship the deity and purify himself in a sacred river or tank, perhaps after a ceremonial head shaving; he may also circumambulate the holy spot, give alms, listen to religious discourses, and chant religious songs. Although not a traditionally recognized means of attaining release, pilgrimage is considered a good way to gain religious merit and specific boons within a life lived according to caste and class duties.

Especially important centers of pilgrimage for the followers of Shiva are the twelve most sacred lingas, known as the "Lingas of Light." Some are natural formations (stalagmites, for example, worshiped in caves); others are housed in constructed temples. The origin of each is the subject of a myth. The Linga of Light at Kedarnath high in the Himalayas, for example, was said to have been given by Shiva as a boon to the devout sages Nara and Narayana. The one at Rameshwaram on an island at the southern tip of the country is believed to have been established by the god Rama to gain absolution from his sin of killing Ravana, who though an evil demon, was nonetheless a Brahman.

Certain spots are believed to be sacred places where special access to Shiva may be gained. Pilgrimages to these sites—often located in such remote areas as mountaintops and the sources of rivers—are undertaken to enlist Shiva's aid in obtaining benefits in this world and a better existence in the next. The hardships encountered along the way, such as those being endured by these pilgrims as they make a steep climb to a holy site on a hilltop, are believed to increase spiritual discipline and personal purity.

Other Lingas of Light are located at the far extremes of India and in the interior, in remote places and near cities. Indeed, if one were to visit all the Lingas of Light, one would travel the length and breadth of the country: India is Shiva's sacred domain, and his presence pervades every corner of the land.

Other important centers of pilgrimage are the Five Elements Lingas, which are associated with the five elements of existence— earth, water, fire, wind, and ether—the totality of which Shiva embodies. The Five Elements Lingas are all located in South India. Some are quite literally associated with the elements that they represent: the ether linga, for instance, is invisible because it is said to be composed entirely of ether, a transparent, essential substance.

Pilgrimages to the sites of the Lingas of Light or the Five Elements Lingas, as indeed to any spot sacred to Shiva, are believed to bring great rewards. More holy sites in India are associated with Shiva than with any other god. Some of these are easily accessible, while others are very difficult to reach. Travel to one pilgrimage center, Amarnath in Kashmir, is extremely hazardous. At this sacred site, located high in the snow-covered Himalayas, about 13,000 feet above sea level, is a cavern where Shiva is worshiped in the shape of an ice linga formed by water that drips naturally from the cave's ceiling. According to tradition, the ice cone starts to form at the beginning of every lunar month. It continues to grow until the middle of the month, when it miraculously begins to decrease in size, and by the end of each month, it vanishes. The process is repeated again the next month—and every month thereafter.

Since Amarnath is snowbound most of the year, pilgrimages are usually made in August. The procession starts out from the city of Srinagar, and includes thousands of followers from all castes and classes. Sudden snowstorms and the rigors of the 142-mile trek to the cave on the mountain and back take their toll, often causing a number of deaths among the pilgrims, who in their devotion to Shiva will risk everything. To die on this pilgrimage almost certainly assures one of a better life to come.

Most important Hindu holy places and pilgrimage sites are associated with specific legends and myths. One legend tells of a cow that attained release by worshiping the linga housed in a Shiva temple. This stone carving from South India (eighth century), showing a cow licking a Shiva linga in adoration, is believed to represent this legend. (Los Angeles County Museum of Art, Gift of Mr. and Mrs. Harry Lenart)

Along the route, devotees stop at sacred spots to bathe and to perform rituals. Their path takes them higher and higher into the mountains until eventually they are walking on snow. About four miles from the cave, they leave behind any excess baggage, and begin the last stage in the steep ascent, where, at last, they behold the ice linga in the cave.

Pilgrims who throng these pilgrimage sites return to their families and their daily lives spiritually refreshed. There is one supremely sacred place in India, however, where people hope to

Benares is Shiva's city and one of the holiest pilgrimage sites in India. Located on the banks of the sacred river Ganges, it is filled with shrines and temples to Shiva and to the other gods. Nothing in Benares is far from the Ganges: pilgrims, holy men, and funeral processions—all are ultimately drawn to the river's purifying waters.

go at the end of their lives—to die. This is Benares, or as it is known in the texts, Kashi, the City of Light, the luminous city. Benares is Shiva's city. One of the most ancient towns in India, it is, perhaps, one of the oldest living cities in the world. Hindus believe that if they die in Benares they will instantly attain release: there, at the moment of death, Shiva is said to reveal a mantra that liberates all believers.

Benares is imbued with Shiva's presence, and to a devout Hindu it is like no other place on earth. Temples to Shiva are found throughout the city, but, perhaps the most important focus of a pilgrim's journey there is the sacred river Ganges, which flows past it. The slightest touch of this river offers liberation from all evil deeds of the past. To reach its banks, one must thread one's way through an endless maze of narrow lanes and

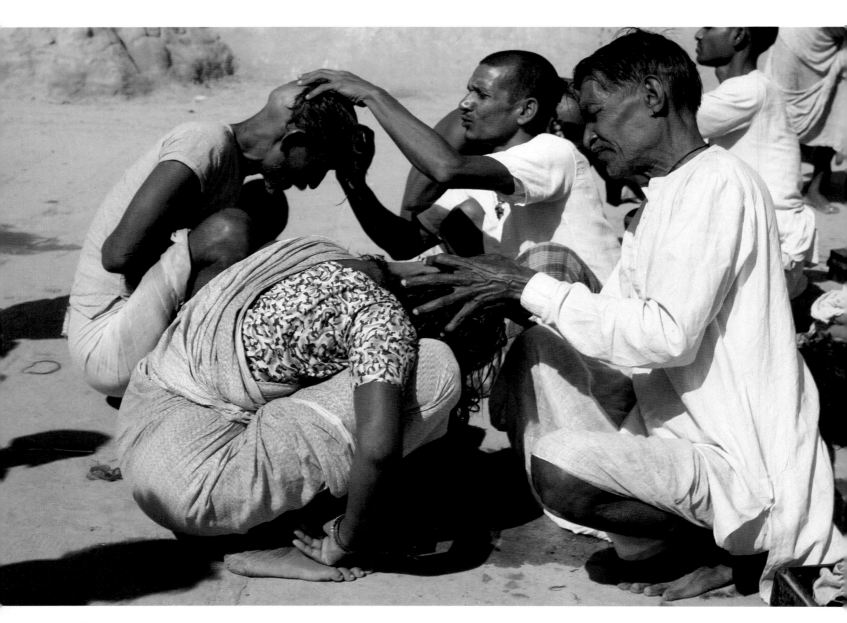

alleyways, choked with people, horse-drawn carts, and cows. And, then, suddenly, with a burst of light, one is upon it—the wide crescent-shaped expanse of the Ganges stretching as far as the eye can see. At sunrise, pilgrims flock to the river to take their morning baths. Day and night, corpses are cremated at burning grounds along the river, and various rites, particularly those honoring dead ancestors, are performed there daily. Besides bathing in the river, pilgrims visit the many temples and shrines of Benares, one of the holiest being the golden Vishvanatha Temple, which houses a Linga of Light. In hopes of attaining material and spiritual rewards, they also circumambulate the city by walking down Panchakroshi Road, which is many miles long and encircles Benares and some of the surrounding countryside.

Mantras, yantras, images, pujas, and pilgrimages to holy places constitute the ways to Shiva for most people, particularly those householders who live their lives according to the rites and rules of caste and class. By performing these rituals, they can be sure of access to Shiva and of gaining his help in solving problems and in leading a life properly so that release from the endless cycles of existence may eventually be attained.

Intense love for a personal god is a more spontaneous way to Shiva. This is a path often followed by people of lower castes because their social position prevents them from participating in or performing many rituals; they hope that Shiva will be moved by their love to grant their requests and the ultimate reward of more immediate release. But the way of intense love is also followed by people who wish a more personally expressive

Throughout the day, pilgrims to Benares bathe in the holy and purifying waters of the Ganges. The young man (left), completely absorbed in devotion, makes a gesture of deep reverence to the gods before immersing himself in the river. The old woman (right), surrounded by other bathers, presents the holy river with an offering of flowers and a lighted oil lamp.

spiritual life. By those who follow the path of love solely, ritual duties are somewhat ignored or, at the most, thought to be of lesser importance. For them, salvation and help with concrete matters can neither be bought nor forced: they come only as gifts granted by Shiva to the devotee in response to his utter surrender and ecstatic love.

Perhaps the most moving expressions of this intense love are the hymns composed by poet-saints known as Nayanars who,

Hindus believe that if one dies in Benares, the soul will be released from the endless rounds of death and rebirth. People from all over India come to spend their last days in the city; funeral processions are a frequent sight, and at some burning places along the river, such as the one seen here, corpses are cremated day and night.

starting in the sixth century of this era, spread a popular worship of Shiva in South India. Their hymns brought together myths of Shiva from sacred writings, local legends, and the saints' own experiences and were written in the regional language Tamil rather than the classical Indian language Sanskrit. Certain of these poets left such an enormous impact that they themselves are now regarded as saints, and images of them are honored in temples.

The religion of Shiva is not, however, all ritual and devotion: schools of complex philosophy, developed over many centuries, and the practices of rigorous spiritual discipline are also associated with it. For a person who possesses capacities for self-realization, and who has in some way renounced the everyday world, there exists one more way to Shiva and release—the path of knowledge. By meditating upon the Great God, the embodiment of the Absolute, such a person comes to know that his true self and the ultimate reality are one, and that the apparent differences between them are only illusory. Such a difficult realization, however, cannot usually be attained without the assistance of a spiritual teacher, a Shiva guru.

The guru is regarded by his followers as a human manifestation of Shiva, for having attained oneness with the Absolute, he lives in continual union with the Great God. Acting as a spiritual guide, he leads his disciples to Shiva and to release with an organized spiritual discipline that is adjusted to suit each person's capacities and potential. His disciples, in turn, make a complete and total surrender to him. During the course of their meditations, some of them will fully realize that they, the guru, and Shiva, are one. Devotion and ritual are both ways to Shiva; but following the guru is the most personal and most mysterious path. For in complete surrender to him, that is, to Shiva incarnate, lies the hope for an end to pain and the promise of release—not in the next life, but in this one.

The trident is an attribute sacred to Shiva. In this painting from Jaipur (late eighteenth century), two devotees, each waving a fly whisk, worshipfully attend the trident; offerings lie before it and oil lamps rest at its sides. Above, the sun and the moon, whose movements define time and life, stand in attendance. Swastikas—ancient and auspicious Indian symbols—decorate the background. The eyes of the Great God—male and female, creator and destroyer, the totality of existence—confront the viewer with a powerful, hypnotic gaze. (Collection Navin Kumar)

Glossary

Agni. Aryan god of fire.

artha. Worldly success; one of the four basic aims of Hindu life.

Aryans. Nomadic horsemen and cattle breeders who originally lived near the Caspian Sea and began to conquer India sometime before 1000 B.C.

avatar ("descent"). An incarnation by the Hindu god Vishnu to save the world from evil and to restore order; Vishnu is traditionally said to have ten avatars.

Brahma. Four-headed Hindu god of creation.

Brahman. Member of the first, or priestly, Hindu class.

Buddha. Title applied to Shakyamuni (563?–?483 B.C.) when he attained Enlightenment and began to preach the doctrines later known as Buddhism; considered by Hindus to be the ninth incarnation of the Hindu god Vishnu.

Buddhists. Followers of the teachings of the Buddha.

caste. One of the homogeneous groups within the four great classes of the Indian social structure. Elaborate and strict rules govern all relations among the castes.

Devi. One of the three supreme Hindu gods, the Great Goddess who embodies universal energy and who has many creative-destructive forms.

dharma. Moral and religious duty; one of the four basic aims of Hindu life.

Durga. Name of the Hindu goddess Devi in a terrific, or destructive, form.

Five Ambrosias. The five nectars—milk, curds, clarified butter, honey, and sugar—poured over a symbol or effigy of a deity during the Hindu worship ceremony.

Five Elements Lingas. Five important lingas at five pilgrimage sites in South India, each associated with one of the elements of existence—fire, wind, earth, water, and ether.

forest dweller. A man at the third of the four stages of an ideal Hindu life who, retiring to a forest hermitage with his wife, leads an ascetic life of meditation and contemplation.

Ganesha. Elephant-headed Hindu god who creates and removes obstacles; god of wisdom; usually regarded as the son of Shiva; his mount and animal form is the rat.

Gayatri. Verse from the Rig-Veda repeated by Hindus during daily devotions.

guru. A spiritual guide or teacher invested with the right to give initiation.

Indra. Chief of the Aryan gods; later, in Hinduism, relegated to minor role as a rain god and guardian of the Eastern Quarter of the universe.

Jains. Followers of an Indian religious doctrine founded by Vardhamana Mahavira in the sixth century B.C.

Kali. Name of the Hindu goddess Devi in a bloodthirsty, all-destroying form.

Kalkin. Tenth incarnation (the one to come) of the Hindu god Vishnu; believed to be a future world savior.

kama. Pursuit of love; one of the four basic aims of Hindu life.

karma ("action, deed"). According to Hindu beliefs, the full effect of actions performed in this life or in a former one, that determines one's present and future character and form.

93

Karttikeya. Six-faced god of war and son of the Hindu god Shiva; his mount and animal form is the peacock.

Krishna. Eighth incarnation of the Hindu god Vishnu, the center of an extremely popular Hindu devotional cult.

Kshatriya. Member of the second, or warrior and ruler, Hindu class.

linga. Sign or symbol of the Hindu god Shiva; a representation of his erect phallus and of his aspect as the Axis of Existence; main object of worship in a Shiva temple.

Lingas of Light. The twelve most sacred lingas in India, especially important centers of pilgrimage for followers of the Hindu god Shiva.

Mahisha. Demon killed by the Hindu goddess Durga when he attempted to leave his water buffalo form and assume the form of a man.

mantra. A sound or group of sounds (which may or may not have a conventional meaning) that are recited during Hindu worship and meditation, often almost endlessly, to call up an aspect of a deity.

moksha. Release from the empty pleasures and pain of everyday life so that one might fully realize and merge with the Absolute and escape endless death and rebirth; one of the four basic aims of Hindu life; the ultimate goal and purpose of existence.

mudra. Ritual hand gestures used in Hindu worship and meditation that establish a firmer bond between the devotee and the god.

Muslims. Followers of the Islamic faith.

Nandi. The Hindu god Shiva's bull mount and animal form.

Parsis. Followers in India of the national religion of ancient Iran, Zoroastrianism.

Parvati. Gracious, benevolent wife of the Hindu god Shiva; her mount and animal form is the lion.

puja. Ritual worship of images of the Hindu gods.

Rama. Hero of the Ramayana, a great Hindu epic; seventh incarnation of the Hindu god Vishnu and the center of a popular Hindu devotional cult.

Rama with a Battle-Ax. Sixth incarnation of the Hindu god Vishnu.

Rig-Veda. A collection of hymns composed in verse, the first of the four sacred texts of the ancient Aryan religion, which are also regarded as holy by Hindus.

Rudra. Aryan deity; the Great Archer and bestower of healing herbs; later one of the components of the Hindu god Shiva.

sannyasi. A begging wanderer at the fourth and final stage of an ideal Hindu life who, abandoning all worldly ties, wanders homeless in search of ultimate Truth.

Shiva. One of the three supreme Hindu gods.

Shudra. Member of the fourth, or servant, Hindu class.

Sikhs. Followers of a reformist Hindu sect founded in the late fifteenth and early sixteenth century A.D.

Vaishya. Member of the third, or merchant and farming, Hindu class.

Vishnu. One of the three supreme Hindu gods, a kind deity who works continuously for the world's welfare by appearing in various incarnations, or avatars, to save the world from evil demons.

yantra. An abstract geometrical figure that captures an aspect of a Hindu deity and diagrams his basic energies; used for meditation upon and worship of the god.

yoga. A system of spiritual and physical exercises meant to still the mind so that one may attain union with the Absolute.

For Further Reading

BASHAM, A. L. *The Wonder That Was India: A Survey of the History and Culture of the Indian Sub-Continent before the Coming of the Muslims.* 1954. Reprint. New York: Taplinger Publishing Co., 1968.

BROWN, W. NORMAN. *Man in the Universe: Some Cultural Continuities in Indian Thought.* Berkeley and Los Angeles: University of California Press, 1966.

HOPKINS, THOMAS. *The Hindu Religious Tradition.* Belmont, Calif.: Dickenson Publishing Co., 1971.

KRAMRISCH, STELLA. *The Hindu Temple.* 2 vols. 1946. Reprint. Delhi: Motilal Banarsidass, 1976.

KRAMRISCH, STELLA. *The Art of India: Traditions of Indian Sculpture, Painting, and Architecture.* London: The Phaidon Press, 1954.

KRAMRISCH, STELLA. *Manifestations of Shiva.* Philadelphia: Philadelphia Museum of Art, 1981.

KRAMRISCH, STELLA. *The Presence of Śiva.* Princeton: Princeton University Press, 1981.

O'FLAHERTY, WENDY DONIGER. *Asceticism and Eroticism in the Mythology of Śiva.* London: Oxford University Press, 1973.

O'FLAHERTY, WENDY DONIGER, ed. and trans. *Hindu Myths: A Sourcebook Translated from the Sanskrit.* Baltimore: Penguin Books, 1975.

RAMANUJAN, A.K., ed. and trans. *Speaking of Śiva.* Baltimore: Penguin Books, 1973.

ROWLAND, BENJAMIN. *The Art and Architecture of India: Buddhist—Hindu—Jain.* Rev. ed. Baltimore: Penguin Books, 1977.

ZIMMER, HEINRICH. *Myths and Symbols in Indian Art and Civilization.* Edited by Joseph Campbell. 1946. Reprint. Princeton: Princeton University Press, 1971.

Photographic Credits